CHICKE

MW00927957

CHICKEN BREAST a cookbook

CHICKEN BREAST

a cookbook

By

Colin Simpson

© 2018 Cape Neddick Cookbooks
4th Edition

ISBN-13: 978-1497428447
ISBN-10: 1497428440

DEDICATION

This book is dedicated to my friends and family. Thank you for your support.

TABLE OF CONTENTS

About the book
About the author
Introduction
The recipes

02. Creamy Bourbon Chicken
04. Fried Chicken Salad
06. Salsa Chicken
07. Mild Spice Chicken with Peas and Corn
08. Chicken Enchilada Dish
09. Apricot Chicken
10. Chicken Cacciatore
12. Pineapple Chicken Stir-Fry
14. Chicken Parmesan
16. Cranberry Chicken
18. Lemon Ginger Chicken
20. Chicken Quesadillas
22. Chicken Caesar Salad
24. Rosemary Chicken Salad Sandwiches
26. Caribbean Chicken Stew
28. Chicken Biryani
30. Pita Chicken Sandwiches
32. Balsamic Chicken and Pears
34. Chicken Marsala
36. Curried Chicken and Rice
38. Chicken Fajitas
40. Chicken Curry
42 Chicken Cheese Cranberry Panini
44. Chicken Fajita Roll Ups
45. Chicken Caesar Pasta Salad
46. Mediterranean Chicken Salad Sandwich
48. Chicken and Potato Salad
50. Chicken and Asparagus Salad
52. Chicken with Orange and Garlic

54. Chicken with Zucchini and Tomatoes

56. Chicken Souvlaki

58. Chicken Marsala #2

60. Fried Chicken Fingers

62. Creamy Garlic Pasta Chicken Veg

64. Lemon & Dill Chicken

Bonus salad recipes

66. Chicken Waldorf salad

68. Cranberry Tarragon Chicken Salad

70. Orzo Chicken Salad

72. Chicken Caesar Salad

74. Rosemary Chicken Salad

76. Chicken Potato Salad

78. Chicken Asparagus Salad

80. Cassie's Chicken Salad

Bonus recipes

82. Chicken broth

83. Salsa

84. Guacamole

85. Mayonnaise

About The Book

Dear Friends!

Welcome to Chicken Breast a cookbook! This book features my favorite recipes that can be cooked in 30 minutes or less using boneless skinless chicken, healthy fresh ingredients and a skillet. These great tasting recipes are quick and easy, offering the perfect solution to busy families with simple, healthy alternatives to fast food restaurants.

More than a third of American adults and approximately 17% of children are considered obese* and this figure is expected to continue to rise dramatically. Changing to healthier food alternatives, along with regular exercise, can help stop this worrying trend and prevent obesity-related health concerns such as heart disease, type-2 diabetes and stroke.

Chicken is a wonderfully versatile and protein-enriched food with many health benefits. Cooked in lean form, chicken can help reduce the intake of solid fats while improving nutrient absorption. It can help lower cholesterol and improve metabolism for a healthy heart, it can aid in building muscles which in turn protects bones and its minerals can help boost the immune system.

Best of all, chicken is cost effective and easy to prepare; from a hearty chicken soup in winter to a light summer salad; from a simple stir fry to a delicious cacciatore. Most recipes can be made in advance and frozen for added convenience. With a wide selection of tasty dishes for every occasion, chicken can become as popular in your house as it is in ours without ever being boring!

Happy healthy cooking!

Colin Simpson.

About the author

Colin is a professional cook and former restaurateur who resides on the beautiful coast of Southern Maine in New England. From the moment he was the first male to take cooking classes in his high school in Edinburgh, Scotland, Colin has not stopped developing his passion for cooking. Having travelled extensively, his constant focus has been learning new recipes and cooking techniques around the globe.

Colin's first cookbook **Salmon a cookbook** became a best seller within a week of its release. Colin has always enjoyed sharing his tasty dishes with family and friends and now as a successful author he continues to write to share his favorite recipes with a wider audience.

Other books in Colin's 'a cookbook' series:

SALMON a cookbook
LAMB a cookbook
CHICKEN BREAST a cookbook
Soup of the Day

http://www.amazon.com/Colin-Simpson/e/B00DYQNMGG

Introduction

Good organization is key to successful cooking, to avoid mistakes and save time. I have a simple process I use with all recipes which is probably similar to yours, but thought I would share it with you.

After reading the entire recipe through, I ensure all my ingredients and utensils are laid out in place. I pre-heat the oven if required and then do all the prep, following the recipe instructions in the listed order. When ready to cook, I set the timer. Being prepared makes cooking easy, more fun and saves time!

The recipes are displayed so you never need to turn a page. There is even space at the end of the recipes for you to write your own notes.

CHICKEN BREAST

a cookbook

The Recipes:

Creamy Bourbon Chicken

Prep: 10 min - Cook: 15 min - Serves Four

Ingredients:

1 lb. chicken breast - cut into 4 pieces

8 ounces mushrooms - sliced

1 small onion - sliced

1 cup light cream

1/2 cup all-purpose flour

1/2 cup peas

1/3 cup bourbon

3 tablespoons butter

2 tablespoons olive oil

salt and ground black pepper to taste

Directions:

1. Sprinkle chicken breasts with salt and pepper; coat in flour, set aside.

2. Cook peas per package instructions, set to side.

3. Heat olive oil and butter in skillet, add chicken, sauté chicken on both sides till cooked and browned - about 10 minutes. Baste chicken with small amounts of bourbon every few minutes as it cooks. Remove chicken from skillet and set to side.

4. Add sliced mushrooms and sliced onion to skillet, cook for about 3 minutes, stirring constantly, then add cream and peas. Simmer till sauce begins to thicken, then add salt and pepper to taste. Add chicken to sauce, simmer one more minute.

5. Serve immediately.

Served With Suggestion:

Whole grain rice, baked potato, vegetable of your choice, or salad.

Fried Chicken Salad

Prep: 10 min - Cook: 10 min - Serves Four

Ingredients:

Fried chicken fingers

1 head iceberg lettuce

3 eggs - boiled - cooled - cut into wedges

1 cup shredded cheese - cheddar or Mexican blend

1 cup cherry tomatoes

1 cup croutons

1 cucumber - sliced

1 green pepper - sliced

1/2 cup ranch dressing

Directions:

1. Prepare fried chicken as per recipe - Fried Chicken Fingers recipe.

2. Tear lettuce into bite size pieces in large bowl; add cheese, tomato, green pepper and cucumber.

3. Arrange salad on four individual plates.

4. Top with egg and chicken, then dressing.

5. Serve immediately.

Served With Suggestion:

Whole wheat bread rolls.

Salsa Chicken

Prep: 10 min - Cook: 20 min - Serves Four

Ingredients:

1 lb. chicken breast - cut into 4 pieces

1 can black beans - drained

1 cup chunky salsa

1 cup cheddar cheese—low fat—shredded

1/2 cup fat free chicken broth

1 tablespoon apple cider vinegar

1 tablespoon olive oil

Directions:

1. Heat oil in a large skillet over medium heat and brown chicken for 4 minutes on each side.

2. Add the beans, salsa, chicken broth and apple cider vinegar to chicken, cover and simmer for 10 minutes.

3. Top with cheese - broil till cheese melts.

4. Serve immediately.

Served with suggestion:

Rice, green salad and whole wheat bread rolls.

Mild Spice Chicken with Peas and Corn

Prep: 10 min - Cook: 30 min - Serves Four

Ingredients:

1 lb. chicken breast - cut into 4 pieces

1 cup cheddar cheese—low fat—shredded

2 tomatoes - diced

Combine the following ingredients in a bowl:

1 1/2 cups instant white rice - uncooked

2 cups chicken broth - fat free

1/3 cup mayonnaise

1/4 cup frozen peas

1/4 cup frozen corn

1 tablespoon chili powder

1 tablespoon olive oil

1/4 teaspoon salt

Directions:

1. Put the bowl contents into skillet, place chicken on top. Bring to boil, cover and simmer on low heat for 20 minutes.

2. Top with cheese - broil till cheese melts.

3. Garnish with diced tomato.

4. Serve immediately.

Chicken Enchilada Dish

Prep: 5 min - Cook: 10 min - Serves Four

Ingredients:

1 lb. chicken breast - shredded

12 corn tortillas - cut into bite size pieces

1 cup Mexican blend shredded cheese

1/3 cup red onion - finely chopped

1 green chili - finely chopped

1 tablespoon olive oil

Combine the following ingredients in a bowl:

1 can diced tomatoes and green chilies - 10 oz.

1 can red enchilada sauce - 10 oz.

1 cup tomato sauce

Directions:

1. Put oil in skillet, add chicken and brown, next add tortilla pieces, onion and chili, and stir well. Cook for 5 minutes over medium-high heat, stirring often.

2. Pour bowl mix over chicken, stir well.

3. Sprinkle top with 1/2 cup cheese.

4. Cover skillet and continue to cook for 5 minutes, stirring occasionally.

5. Sprinkle with remaining cheese.

6. Serve immediately.

Apricot Chicken

Prep: 10 min - Cook: 15 min - Serves Four

Ingredients:

1 lb. chicken breast - cut into 4 pieces

1 tablespoon olive oil

Combine the following ingredients in a small bowl:

1 jar apricot preserves - 12 oz.

1/2 cup low salt chicken broth

2 tablespoons fresh ginger - minced

2 garlic cloves - crushed

salt and pepper to taste

Directions:

1. Heat oil in skillet over medium heat. Brown chicken on both sides - about 5 minutes.

2. Pour over small bowl mix over chicken, cover and simmer for 5 - 10 minutes.

3. Serve immediately.

Served with suggestion:

Serve over white rice. Garden salad, fruit salad and your choice of bread.

Chicken Cacciatore

Prep: 10 min - Cook: 20 min - Serves Four

Ingredients:

1 lb. chicken breast - cut into 1-inch cubes

1 can diced tomatoes - 14.5 oz.

1 can tomato sauce - 8 oz.

8 oz. mushrooms - sliced

1 large onion - cut into strips

1 large green pepper - cut into strips

1 garlic clove - minced - about 1 teaspoon

2 teaspoons Italian seasoning

2 tablespoons olive oil

1 tablespoon tomato paste

Combine the following ingredients in a bowl:

1 tablespoon flour

1 teaspoon salt

1/4 teaspoon black pepper

Directions:

1. Coat chicken evenly in bowl mixture.

2. Heat 1 tablespoon of oil in skillet over medium heat. Add chicken and cook for 5 minutes on each side, or until lightly browned, then remove chicken from skillet.

3. Heat 1 tablespoon of olive oil in skillet, add mushrooms, onion and peppers. Cook for 5 minutes on medium heat.

4. Add diced tomatoes, tomato sauce, tomato paste, garlic and Italian seasoning to skillet. Bring to boil, stirring frequently.

5. Return chicken to skillet, reduce heat to low, cover and simmer for 10 minutes.

6. Serve immediately.

Served with suggestion:

Serve over your favorite pasta with garlic bread.

Pineapple Chicken Stir-Fry

Prep: 10 min - Cook: 20 min - Serves Four

Ingredients:

2 cups cooked white rice

1 cup pineapple chunks - drained - save drained juice

1 cup snow peas - cut half lengthwise

2/3 cups green onion - green part only - chopped

1 green pepper - cut into strips

1 carrot - sliced

2 tablespoons sesame oil

1: Combine the following ingredients in a bowl:

1lb chicken breast - cut into 1-inch cubes

2 teaspoons soy sauce - low sodium

2 teaspoons rice vinegar

1/4 teaspoon ground ginger

2: Sauce: combine the following ingredients in a small bowl:

1/4 cup pineapple juice

4 garlic gloves - minced

3 tablespoons soy sauce - low sodium

2 tablespoons chicken broth - low sodium

1 teaspoon corn starch

Directions:

1. Combine first bowl ingredients and set aside. Combine second bowl ingredients to make sauce and set aside.

2. Heat 1 tablespoon of sesame oil in skillet over medium heat. Add carrot and green pepper, stir for 3 minutes. Add snow peas, stir another 2 minutes. Then remove vegetables from skillet.

3. Add 1 tablespoon of sesame oil to skillet, add chicken and stir till chicken is cooked - about 4 minutes.

4. Return vegetables to pan, add onion and stir for 2 minutes. Stir sauce and pour into skillet, and add pineapple. Stir till sauce thickens - about 2 minutes.

5. Serve immediately over cooked rice.

Served with suggestion:

Your favorite salad and bread rolls.

Chicken Parmesan

Prep: 5 min - Cook: 20 min - Serves Four

Ingredients:

1 lb. chicken breast - cut into 4 pieces

1 can tomato sauce - 14.5 oz.

1/2 cup seasoned bread crumbs

1 egg - beaten

4 slices mozzarella cheese

1 tablespoon olive oil

1 tablespoon tomato paste

1 tablespoon parmesan cheese - grated

1 teaspoon Italian seasoning

1/8 teaspoon salt

1/8 teaspoon black pepper

Directions:

1. Pound chicken to flatten then sprinkle with salt and pepper.

2. Dip chicken in egg, then coat in breadcrumbs.

3. Heat oil in skillet over medium heat, add chicken and cook till browned on both sides - about 10 minutes. Remove chicken from skillet.

4. Add tomato sauce, tomato paste and Italian seasoning to skillet, sir occasionally and heat till hot.

5. Place chicken on top of tomato sauce in skillet, and place one slice of mozzarella on top each piece of chicken. Cover and cook on medium heat for few minutes, or until cheese melts. Sprinkle parmesan cheese on top. Brown under broiler - optional.

6. Serve immediately.

Served with suggestion:

Spaghetti or ziti and garlic bread.

Cranberry Chicken

Prep: 10 min - Cook: 20 min - Serves Four

Ingredients:

1 lb. chicken breast - cut into 4 pieces

1 tablespoon olive oil

1: Combine the following ingredients in a bowl:

1/4 cup flour

1/2 teaspoon mustard powder

1/2 teaspoon salt

1/2 teaspoon black pepper

2: Combine the following ingredients in a bowl:

1 cup dried cranberries - sweetened

1/2 cup apple juice

1/2 cup chicken stock - low sodium

1 tablespoon Dijon mustard

Directions:

1. Combine first bowl ingredients and set aside. Combine second bowl ingredients and set aside.

2. Pound chicken to flatten and coat chicken well in 1st bowl mix.

3. Heat olive oil in skillet over medium heat. Add chicken and cook for 5 minutes on each side, or until lightly browned. Remove chicken and drain oil from skillet.

3. Add 2nd bowl mix to skillet, reduce heat to low, then add chicken, cover and cook for 5 -10 minutes, stirring sauce occasionally.

4. Serve immediately.

Served with suggestion:

Baked potato, side salad and whole wheat bread rolls.

Lemon Ginger Chicken

Prep: 10 min - Cook: 25 min - Serves Four

Ingredients:

1 lb. chicken breast - cut into 4 pieces

2 teaspoons olive oil

2 tablespoons green onion - sliced

1 lemon - sliced

2 tablespoons parsley - fresh - chopped

1: Combine the following ingredients in a small bowl:

1 tablespoon ginger - fresh - grated

2 teaspoons lemon grind

1/2 teaspoon salt

1/4 teaspoon black pepper

2: Combine the following ingredients in a small bowl:

2 tablespoons lemon juice

2 tablespoons honey

2 tablespoons water

1 tablespoon soy sauce - reduced sodium

Directions:

1. Rub bowl mixture on chicken. Set aside.

2. Heat olive oil in skillet over medium heat. Add chicken and cook for 5 minutes on each side, or until lightly browned.

3. Add second bowl mixture, then reduce heat, cover and simmer for 15 minutes.

4. Top each fillet with lemon slice and parsley.

5. Serve immediately, garnish with green onion.

Served with suggestion:

Serve over bed of rice, garnish with lemon wedges. A green salad and whole wheat bread rolls.

Chicken Quesadillas

Prep: 15 min - Cook: 10 min - Serves Four

Ingredients:

1 lb. chicken breast - chopped

4 flour tortillas—10 inches

8oz Mexican blend cheese—low fat—shredded

2 tomatoes—diced

1 tablespoon olive oil

1 tablespoon butter—softened

2 teaspoons lemon juice

2 teaspoons basil—dried

2 garlic cloves—minced

1/2 teaspoon black pepper

1/8 teaspoon salt

Directions:

1. Heat olive oil in a skillet over medium heat; add garlic and chicken to skillet, sauté till cooked, about 5 minutes.

2. Add basil, salt, pepper and lemon juice to skillet, stir well, and then remove from heat. Put skillet contents into a bowl.

3. Spread Butter on one side of each tortilla. Place tortilla butter side down in skillet.

4. Cover 1/2 of tortilla with 1/2 cup of chicken; sprinkle chicken with diced tomato and 2oz of cheese. Fold tortilla in half.

5. Cook in skillet on medium to low heat for 2 minutes, flip over tortilla and cook another 2 minutes, or until tortilla begins to brown. Repeat process for the other 3 tortillas.

6. Serve immediately.

Served with suggestion:

Serve with a side of salsa and/or guacamole and whole wheat tortilla chips. A green or fruit side salad also compliments these delicious tasting quesadillas.

Chicken Caesar Salad

Prep: 10 min - Cook: 15 min - Serves Four

Ingredients:

1 lb. chicken breast - cut into strips

1 1/2 cups croutons

1 cup caesar dressing—low fat

1/4 cup parmesan cheese—grated

2 romaine lettuce - tear into bite size pieces

1 lemon—cut into 8 wedges

1 tablespoon olive oil

Combine the following ingredients in a small bowl:

1 1/2 teaspoons garlic salt

1 teaspoon lemon pepper seasoning

Directions:

1. Rub small bowl mix on chicken.

2. Heat olive oil in skillet over medium heat. Add chicken and cook for 10 - 15 minutes, or until cooked, stirring often.

3. Cut lettuce into bite size pieces and place in large bowl.

4. Add caesar dressing, parmesan cheese and croutons to

lettuce. Toss until combined well.

5. Divide caesar salad evenly on 4 plates.

6. Place cooked chicken strips on top of salad.

7. Garnish with 2 lemon wedges.

8. Serve immediately.

Served with suggestion:

A side dish of sautéed zucchini and summer squash with whole wheat bread rolls.

Slice 3 large zucchini and 3 large summer squash. Cook with 1 tablespoon of olive oil and 1/2 teaspoon of Italian seasoning in a skillet. Cover and cook for 4-5 minutes over medium heat.

Rosemary Chicken Salad Sandwiches

Prep: 10 min - Cook: 0 min - Serves Four

Ingredients:

8 slices bread - whole grain

4 slices American or cheddar cheese

4 lettuce leaves

Sliced tomato

Combine the following ingredients in a bowl:

1 lb. chicken breast - chopped - cooked - cooled

1/4 cup green onions - chopped

1/4 cup almonds - chopped

1/4 cup yogurt - plain - fat free

1/4 cup mayonnaise - low fat

1 apple - peeled - cored - chopped

1 teaspoon fresh rosemary - chopped

1 teaspoon Dijon mustard

1/8 teaspoon salt

1/8 teaspoon black pepper

Directions:

1. Bread can be toasted if desired.

2. Divide bowl mixture evenly over 4 slices of bread.

3. Top with lettuce, tomato and cheese.

4. Top with slice of bread. Cut sandwiches in 1/2, diagonally.

Served with suggestion:

Side of your favorite green or fruit salad.

Caribbean Chicken Stew

Prep: 10 min - Cook: 20 min - Serves Four

Ingredients:

1 cup white rice

1 can black beans - drained - rinsed - 15 oz.

1 can tomatoes - diced - 14.5 oz.

1/4 cup red wine - dry

2 tablespoons capers

1 cup chopped onion

2 teaspoons olive oil

1 1/2 teaspoons garlic - minced

Combine the following ingredients in a bowl:

1 lb. chicken breast - cut into bite size pieces

1 teaspoon curry powder

1 teaspoon dried thyme

1/2 teaspoon ground allspice

1/2 teaspoon crushed red pepper

1/2 teaspoon cracked black pepper

Directions:

1. While rice is cooking, heat oil in skillet over medium heat. Add onion and garlic, sauté 3 minutes.

2. Add bowl mix to skillet and sauté 4 minutes.

3. Stir in wine, capers, beans, and tomatoes. Cover, reduce heat, and simmer 10 minutes or until tender.

4. Serve immediately over white rice.

Served With Suggestion:

A green salad and whole wheat bread rolls.

Chicken Biryani

Prep: 10 min - Cook: 20 min - Serves Four

Ingredients:

1 lb. chicken breast - cut into bite size pieces

1 can chicken broth - 14 oz. - fat free

2 cups rice - cooked

3 plum tomatoes - chopped

1 onion - medium - chopped

1 cup peas - frozen - thawed

1/3 raisins

1/4 cup - cilantro - fresh - chopped

1/4 cup almonds - sliced

1 jalapeno pepper - seeded - minced

2 garlic cloves - minced

2 teaspoons olive oil

1 1/2 teaspoons garam masala

2 teaspoon ginger - fresh - minced

3/4 teaspoon ground cumin

1/2 teaspoon salt

4 lime wedges

Directions:

1. Put olive oil in a skillet on medium-low heat. Add chicken and sauté for 3-4 minutes. Add the onion and jalapeno, sauté 3 minutes.

2. Add ginger, garam masala, cumin, salt and garlic, sauté 1 minute.

3. Add broth, tomato, peas, rice and raisins, stir well, and bring to boil. Cover, reduce heat, and simmer for 10 minutes.

4. Stir in cilantro and almonds.

5. Serve immediately. Garnish with lime wedges.

Served With Suggestion:

Cucumber and tomato salad.

Dressing: combine 1/3 cup Greek yogurt, 1 tablespoon chopped green onions, 1 teaspoon fresh lemon juice, 1/4 teaspoon ground cumin, 1/8 teaspoon salt, and a dash of ground red pepper. 1 small thinly sliced cucumber, 2 tomatoes, sliced. Cover salad with dressing.

Pita Chicken Sandwiches

Prep: 10 min - Cook: 15 min - Serves Four

Ingredients:

1 lb. chicken breast - cut into bite size pieces

1 onion - medium - sliced thin

1/2 cup yogurt—low fat

1 cucumber - small - shredded

1 tomato - sliced thin

1 tablespoon olive oil

4 pitas

Combine the following ingredients in a bowl:

1 tablespoon wine vinegar

1-1/2 teaspoon chives - chopped

1 teaspoon salt

1/2 teaspoon pepper

Directions:

1. Heat olive oil in a saucepan on medium-low heat. Add chicken and cook for about 5 minutes, still browned. Add onion; cook for another 4 minutes, till chicken is cooked.

2. Remove cooked chicken and onion from skillet, add to bowl mix and stir.

3. Mix cucumber and yoghurt to make sauce.

4. Split pitas to make pockets. Spread sauce inside pitas.

5. Place 1/4 of chicken mixture and tomato into each pocket.

6. Serve immediately.

Served With Suggestion:

Green salad or fruit salad.

Balsamic Chicken and Pears

Prep: 10 min - Cook: 20 min - Serves Four

Ingredients:

1 lb. chicken breast - cut into strips

2 pears, unpeeled, each cut into 8 wedges

1 cup raisins

1 tablespoon olive oil

Combine the following ingredients in a bowl:

1 cup chicken broth - low fat

1 1/2 tablespoons balsamic vinegar

2 teaspoons all-purpose flour

1 teaspoon sugar

Directions:

1. Heat olive oil in a skillet on medium-low heat. Add chicken and cook for about 5 minutes till cooked, stirring often. Remove chicken from skillet and set to side.

2. Add pear wedges to skillet and cook till tender. Add bowl mix and raisins, boil for one minute.

3. Return cooked chicken to skillet, reduce heat and cover for one minute.

4. Serve immediately.

Served With Suggestion:

Rosemary garlic potato wedges and green beans.

Cut potato into wedges. Parboil potato wedges with skin on about 10 minutes. Drain and allow cooling in a bowl of cold water, then drain from cold water. Put 1 tablespoon of olive oil and 2 teaspoons of fresh chopped rosemary in another bowl; add wedges to coat with oil and rosemary. Put potato wedges on a baking sheet, season wedges with garlic powder. Bake in 425 degree preheated oven for 15-20 minutes, turning once during baking. Remove from oven and serve immediately.

Chicken Marsala

Prep: 5 min - Cook: 20 min - Serves Four

Ingredients:

1 lb. chicken breast - cut into strips

1/2 cup mushrooms - sliced

1/2 cup chicken broth

1/2 cup Marsala wine

10 grape tomatoes - halved

1 clove garlic - minced

2 tablespoons green onion - sliced

2 tablespoons butter

1 tablespoon olive oil

1/2 teaspoon dried leaf basil

Combine the following ingredients in a bowl:

4 tablespoons all-purpose flour

1/2 teaspoon salt

1/4 teaspoon ground black pepper

Directions:

1. Heat butter and olive oil in skillet over medium heat.

2. Coat chicken strips in bowl mix, add to skillet and cook till lightly browned, about 3 minutes each side.

3. Add green onion and garlic, cook for one minute, and then add basil, chicken broth and Marsala wine. Bring to boil, reduce heat and simmer for 2 minutes.

4. Add the tomatoes and mushrooms, cover and simmer for 6 minutes - until chicken is cooked.

5. Put chicken on a platter, top with vegetables and sauce.

6. Serve immediately.

Served with suggestion:

Rice, pasta or baby red potato and a side salad.

Curried Chicken and Rice

Prep: 5 min - Cook: 30 min - Serves Six

Ingredients:

1 lb. chicken breast - cut into 1/2 inch pieces

1 1/2 cups chicken broth

1 1/2 cups orange juice

1 1/2 cups frozen peas and carrots

1 cup long-grain rice

4 green onions, thinly sliced

2 tablespoons olive oil

1 tablespoon flour

Combine the following ingredients in a small bowl:

1 tablespoon brown sugar

1 tablespoon curry powder

1/2 teaspoon dry mustard

1/4 teaspoon pepper

1/8 teaspoon salt

Directions:

1. Put 1 tablespoon of bowl mix and flour into a new bowl, add chicken and coat well.

2. Heat oil in skillet, add chicken and cook till chicken is lightly browned - about 4 minutes. Add green onion and cook another minute.

3. Add chicken broth, orange juice, rice and remainder of bowl mix - stir well. Bring to boil, and then reduce heat to low. Cover and cook for 15 minutes.

4. Stir in peas and carrots, cover and simmer another 10 minutes - or till liquids are absorbed.

5. Serve immediately.

Served With Suggestion:

Garden or fruit salad with whole wheat bread rolls.

Chicken Fajitas

Prep: 10 min - Cook: 15 min - Serves Four

Ingredients:

1 lb. chicken breast - cut into thin strips

8 flour tortillas, 6-in each

4 mild green or red chili peppers - sliced

1 sweet red bell pepper - cut into strips

1 sweet green bell pepper - cut into strips

1 zucchini - cut in strips

8 green onions - sliced

1 medium onion - cut in wedges

2 cloves garlic - minced

2 tablespoons olive oil

1/2 cup sour cream

1/2 cup guacamole

Directions:

1. Heat olive oil in skillet and cook chicken strips over high heat, stirring constantly, for 5 minutes or until cooked. Remove chicken and set to side.

2. Add the onion, garlic and chili peppers to the oil in the pan and sauté over high heat for 2 minutes. Add the bell peppers and zucchini - cook over high heat for 4 minutes.

3. Return chicken to skillet and stir well, heat till hot.

4. Serve immediately with warm tortillas, sour cream, guacamole and sliced green onions.

Served With Suggestion:

Rice and refried beans.

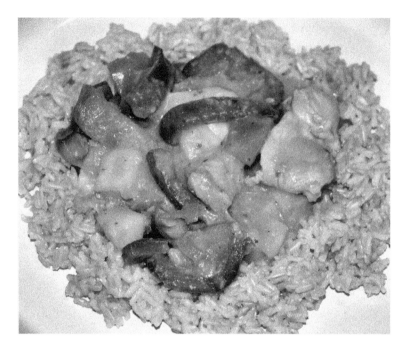

Chicken Curry

Prep: 10 min - Cook: 16 min - Serves Four

Ingredients:

1 lb. chicken breast - cut into 1-inch cubes

1 can coconut milk 12-14 oz. - unsweetened

1 cup canned diced tomatoes

1 medium onion - sliced thin

1 green pepper - sliced thin

1 apple - diced

2 tablespoons tomato paste

1 tablespoon vegetable oil

2 teaspoons curry powder

1/4 teaspoon salt

Directions:

1. Heat oil in skillet over medium heat. Add the onion, green pepper and salt. Cook 5 minutes, stirring often. Stir in curry powder and cook for an additional minute.

2. Stir in coconut milk, tomatoes and tomato paste. Cook for 5 minutes, stirring occasionally.

3. Add the chicken cubes and diced apple, stir well, cook 5 minutes - or until chicken is cooked through.

4. Serve immediately.

Served with suggestion:

Serve over white rice. Garden salad, fruit salad and your choice of bread.

Chicken Cheese Cranberry Panini

Prep: 15 min - Cook: 10 min - Serves Four

Ingredients:

1 lb. chicken breast - cut into thin slices

8 slices Italian bread

8 thin slices white cheddar cheese

4 thin slices cooked ham

1 tablespoon olive oil

1/2 cup mayonnaise

Combine the following ingredients in a small bowl:

1/2 cup Dijon mustard

1/2 cup cranberry sauce

Directions:

1. Heat oil in skillet over medium heat. Brown chicken on both sides - about 5 minutes. Remove chicken and put to side.

2. Spread each slice of bread with small bowl mix. Evenly top four bread slices with chicken, ham and cheese. Top with remaining four slices of bread, bowl-mix-side-down.

3. Spread one tablespoon of mayonnaise on top of each sandwich, put in skillet mayonnaise side down, cook over

medium heat for 2 - 3 minutes, till browned. Spread one tablespoon of mayonnaise on top of each sandwich, turn over, and cook 2 - 3 minutes till browned.

4. Cut sandwiches in half, serve immediately.

Served with suggestion:

Garden salad and/or Potato Salad

Chicken Fajita Roll Ups

Prep: 15 min - Cook: 5 min - Serves Four

Ingredients:

1 lb. chicken breast - cut into strips

1 large green pepper - cut into strips

1 large red bell pepper - cut into strips

1 large red onion, sliced

8 flour tortillas, 6-in each

2 tablespoons olive oil

Combine the following ingredients in a small bowl:

1/2 cup mayonnaise

1/2 cup salsa

Directions:

1. Spread bowl mix evenly over tortillas - put to side.

2. Heat olive oil in skillet and cook chicken strips, pepper and onion over high heat, stirring constantly, for 5 minutes or until cooked.

3. Spoon chicken mixture on center of each tortilla and roll up. Serve immediately.

Chicken Caesar Pasta Salad

Prep: 10 min - Cook: 10 min - Serves Six

Ingredients:

1 (16 ounce) package penne pasta

Combine the following ingredients in a small bowl:

1lb. chicken breast - cooked - diced

1 (16 ounce) bottle Caesar salad dressing

1 red onion - thinly sliced

1 pint cherry tomatoes - halved

1/3 cup parmesan cheese - shredded or shaved

1/2 teaspoon oregano - fresh - chopped

1/2 teaspoon Tabasco sauce

salt and pepper to taste

Directions:

1. Cook penne pasta per package instructions. Rinse under cold water to cool.

2. Heat oil in skillet over medium heat; add chicken and sauté till cooked - about 5 minutes. Drain and let cool. Add to bowl mix, gently toss.

3. Cover and chill till ready to serve.

Mediterranean Chicken Salad Sandwich

Prep: 10 min - Cook: 10 min - Serves Four

Ingredients:

1 lb. chicken breast - chopped

8 slices wheat bread

4 slices Swiss cheese

3/4 cup mayonnaise

4 tablespoons chopped onion

1 tablespoon olive oil

2 garlic cloves - minced

1 teaspoon Italian seasoning

Directions:

1. Heat olive oil in nonstick skillet, add chopped chicken, garlic and Italian seasoning, cook over medium heat - about 5 minutes.

2. Combine cooked chicken, onion and 1/2 cup of mayonnaise in bowl.

3. Spread chicken mixture on 4 slices of bread, top with cheese, and then 4 remaining slices of bread.

4. Spread remaining 1/4 cup of mayonnaise evenly on outside of sandwiches.

5. Cook in nonstick skillet over medium heat, turning once, until bread is toasted and cheese is melted, about 5 minutes.

4. Serve immediately.

Chicken and Potato Salad

Prep: 15 min - Cook: 8 min - Serves Four

Ingredients:

1 lb. chicken breast - chopped

1 lb. potatoes - peeled and cubed

1 tablespoon olive oil

Combine the following ingredients in a bowl:

3/4 cup mayonnaise

1/2 cup grapes - chopped

1/3 cup celery - chopped

1/4 cup onion - chopped

1 apple - peeled and chopped

1 carrot - peeled and chopped

2 tablespoons sofrito

2 tablespoons lime juice

1 tablespoon olive oil

salt and ground black pepper to taste

Directions:

1. Boil cubed potatoes for 8 minutes, remove from heat,

drain and set to side to allow cooling.

2. Heat olive oil in skillet and cook chicken for 4 minutes or until cooked. Set to side.

3. Combine remaining ingredients in a bowl, add cooked chicken and cooked potatoes.

4. Serve at room temperature or chilled.

Served with suggestion:

Green salad and whole wheat bread rolls.

Chicken and Asparagus Salad

Prep: 15 min - Cook: 10 min - Serves Four

Ingredients:

1 lb. chicken breast - cut into 1-inch cubes

8 cups mixed salad greens

12 oz. asparagus - cut into 2-inch pieces

1 cup cherry tomatoes - halved

1/2 cup water

1 tablespoon olive oil

Dressing: combine the following ingredients in a small bowl:

1/2 cup mayonnaise

1/2 cup sour cream

1/4 cup green onion - thinly sliced

1 tablespoon chopped fresh basil leaves

1 tablespoon lemon juice

1/4 teaspoon grated lemon peel

salt and ground black pepper to taste

Directions:

1. Make dressing and chill till ready to serve.

2. Heat olive oil in skillet and cook chicken for 5 minutes or until cooked. Set to side.

3. Bring to boil 1/2 cup water to boil in small saucepan, add asparagus, cover and cook for 4 minutes. Drain and rinse with cold water.

4. In a large salad bowl, combine greens, chicken and tomatoes. Arrange salad onto four plates and top with chilled dressing.

5. Serve immediately.

Served With Suggestion:

Whole wheat bread rolls.

Chicken with Orange and Garlic

Prep: 5 min - Cook: 25 min - Serves Four

Ingredients:

1 lb. chicken breast - cut into 4 pieces

1/4 cup chicken broth - fat free

1/4 cup orange juice

2 green onions - thinly sliced

8 cloves garlic - minced

2 tablespoons fresh parsley - minced

1 tablespoon olive oil

salt and ground black pepper to taste

Directions:

1. Pat chicken dry. Sprinkle with salt and pepper.

2. Heat olive oil in skillet over medium heat and add chicken, green onion, and garlic, sauté about 5 minutes - or till cooked. Remove cooked chicken and put to side.

3. Add chicken broth, orange juice and 1 tablespoon of parsley to skillet; boil for 2 - 3 minutes to allow sauce to reduce. Add chicken, cover, lower heat and simmer for 10 minutes.

4. Serve immediately, garnish with remaining parsley.

Served with suggestion:

Homemade Red Potato oven fries and green beans.
Garnish with orange wedges.

Cut 4 red potatoes into wedges-leave skin on, parboil for 6
minutes. Run wedges under cold water to cool them. Put 1
tablespoon olive oil in a bowl, add wedges, gently stir to
coat wedges with oil. Put wedges on baking sheet, sprinkle
wedges with a garlic salt. Bake fries in 425 degree
preheated oven for 20 minutes, turn wedges over once
during baking.

Chicken with Zucchini and Tomatoes

Prep: 5 min - Cook: 16 min - Serves Four

Ingredients:

1 lb. chicken breast - cut into 4 pieces

4 tomatoes - sliced

4 zucchini - medium - thinly sliced

1/2 cup chicken broth

4 slices Mozzarella cheese

2 tablespoons flour

1 tablespoon olive oil

1/2 teaspoon Cajun seasoning

salt and ground black pepper to taste

Directions:

1. Pat chicken dry, sprinkle with salt, pepper and Cajun seasoning, then coat with flour.

2. Heat olive oil in skillet over medium heat, add chicken and brown on both sides - about 5 minutes.

3. Add chicken broth to skillet, cover and simmer for 5 minutes, then add zucchini, cover and simmer for another 5 minutes.

4. Add tomato, simmer uncovered for 5 minutes, then top chicken with cheese, and allow cheese to melt, about 1 minute.

5. Serve immediately.

Served with suggestion:

Baked Potato and green salad.

Chicken Souvlaki

Prep: 10 min - Cook: 6 min - Serves Four

Ingredients:

1 lb. chicken breast - cut into strips

4 soft pita's - whole wheat - cut in half

2 tomatoes - thinly sliced

1 onion - thinly sliced

1 green bell pepper - thinly sliced

2 garlic cloves - minced

1 tablespoon olive oil

1 teaspoon oregano - fresh - chopped

salt and ground black pepper to taste

Dressing: combine the following ingredients in a small bowl:

1/2 cup cucumber - grated

1/4 cup Greek yogurt

1/4 cup sour cream

1 tablespoon parsley - fresh - chopped

1/2 teaspoon grated lemon rind

1 teaspoon fresh lemon juice

Directions:

1. Make dressing in small bowl, put in fridge while cooking chicken.

2. Heat 2 teaspoons olive oil in skillet over medium heat, sprinkle chicken with salt and pepper to taste, add chicken to skillet and brown - about 5 minutes, or till done. Remove from pan.

3. Add one teaspoon olive oil to skillet, and then add onion and bell pepper, sauté for 3 minutes. Add chicken, oregano and garlic, cook one more minute.

4. Serve immediately with warm pita, tomato and dressing.

Chicken Marsala #2

Prep: 5 min - Cook: 15 min - Serves Four

Ingredients:

1 lb. chicken breast - cut into 4 pieces - pounded 1/4 inch thick

1 cup mushrooms - sliced

1/2 cup Marsala wine

1/4 cup cooking sherry

4 tablespoons butter

4 tablespoons olive oil

Combine the following ingredients in a small bowl:

1/4 cup flour

1/2 teaspoon dried oregano

1/2 teaspoon salt

1/4 teaspoon ground black pepper

Directions:

1. Coat chicken in small bowl mixture.

2. Heat olive oil and butter in skillet over medium heat, add chicken and lightly brown both sides, then add mushrooms, wine and sherry. Cover and simmer chicken for 10 minutes, turning once.

3. Serve immediately.

Served With Suggestion:

Baked potato and vegetable of your choice.

Fried Chicken Fingers

Prep: 5 min - Cook: 8 min - Serves Four

Ingredients:

1 lb. chicken breast - cut into strips

1 cup vegetable oil

Combine the following ingredients in a small bowl:

1 cup all-purpose flour

1/2 tablespoon red pepper flakes

1 teaspoon salt

1/2 teaspoon black pepper

1/2 teaspoon garlic salt

1/2 teaspoon onion powder

Combine the following ingredients in a small bowl:

2 eggs

1/4 cup milk

Directions:

1. Heat oil in skillet on medium heat.

2. Coat each piece of chicken with flour mixture, then egg mixture, then another coat of flour mixture.

3. Fry until golden brown - about 8 minutes.

4. Drain on paper towel for a few minutes, and then serve.

Served With Suggestion:

Your choice of dip, potato or salad.

Creamy Garlic Pasta Chicken & Vegetables

Prep: 10 min - Cook: 20 min - Serves Four

Ingredients:

6 oz. spaghetti - whole-wheat

1lb chicken breast - cut into 1-inch pieces

1 bunch asparagus - trimmed and thinly sliced

1 large red bell pepper - thinly sliced

1/2 cup frozen peas

1/2 cup frozen corn

1/4 cup fresh parsley - chopped

Parmesan cheese - optional.

Combine the following ingredients in a large bowl:

1 1/2 cups Greek yogurt

3 tablespoons lemon juice

1 tablespoon olive oil

1 1/4 teaspoons kosher salt

1/2 teaspoon black pepper

3 cloves garlic - minced

Directions:

1. Cook spaghetti per package instructions, cook for 3 minutes less than package instructions.

2. Then add chicken, asparagus, red bell pepper, peas, and corn to cooking spaghetti. Cook till spaghetti is tender, about 3 to 5 minutes.

3. Drain well.

4. Add pasta mix to large bowl with sauce, toss to coat. Sprinkle with parmesan cheese and garnish with parsley - optional.

5. Serve immediately.

Served With Suggestion:

Whole wheat bread rolls and green salad.

Lemon & Dill Chicken

Prep: 10 min - Cook: 15 min - Serves Four

Ingredients

1 lb. chicken breast - cut into 4 pieces - pounded 1/4 inch thick

1/4 cup onion - chopped fine

1 tablespoons fresh dill - chopped

2 tablespoons white wine

1 tablespoon olive oil

2 cloves garlic - minced

salt and ground black pepper to taste

Combine the following ingredients in a small bowl:

1 cup chicken broth - low sodium

1 tablespoons fresh dill - chopped

2 tablespoons lemon juice

2 teaspoons flour

2 teaspoons lemon zest - freshly grated

Salt and ground black pepper to taste.

Directions

1. Season chicken breasts with salt and pepper.

2. Heat olive oil in skillet over medium heat, add chicken and cook both sides about 3 minutes each, till browned. Remove chicken from pan and set to side.

3. Add wine, onion and garlic to skillet and cook for 1 minute. Add bowl mix, and cook for 4 minutes, stirring constantly.

4. Return chicken to skillet, reduce heat and simmer for 4 minutes.

5. Place chicken on serving plates, top with sauce from skillet and garnish with 1 tablespoon of dill.

6. Serve immediately.

Chicken Waldorf salad

Prep: 10 min - Cook: 15 min - Serves Four

Ingredients:

1 lb. chicken breast - chopped - cooked*

1 lettuce - torn to bite size pieces

1 cup red or green grapes - halved

1 cup celery - sliced

1 red apple - diced

1/3 cup mayonnaise - low fat

1/3 Greek yogurt

2 teaspoons lemon juice

1/4 teaspoon salt

1/4 cup walnuts - chopped

ground black pepper to taste

Directions:

1. In a large bowl whisk the mayonnaise, yogurt, lemon juice and salt.

2. Add cooked chicken, apple, grapes, celery and walnuts. Toss well.

3. Arrange lettuce on serving plates and top with salad.

Sprinkle some ground black pepper on top to taste.

4. Serve immediately.

This dish works well with cooked left over white chicken meat.

*Quick cook chicken method: boil 1 cup chicken stock - low sodium, add chopped chicken, cover and simmer for 5 minutes. Drain chicken and allow cooling for few minutes.

Cranberry Tarragon Chicken Salad

Prep: 10 min - Cook: 5 min - Serves Six

Ingredients:

1 lb. chicken breast - chopped - cooked*

1/4 cup dried cranberries - finely chopped

1/4 cup diced celery

1/4 cup diced red onion

Dressing: combine the following ingredients in a large bowl:

3/4 cup mayonnaise

2 tablespoon lemon juice

2 tablespoons fresh tarragon leaves - chopped

1 tablespoon fresh parsley - chopped

1 tablespoon fresh chives - chopped

1 garlic clove - minced

salt and black pepper to taste

Directions:

1. In a large bowl combine dressing ingredients.

2. Add cooked chicken, cranberries, celery and onion. Toss well.

3. Cover and chill till ready to serve. For best results, chill

for at least 2 hours to allow flavors to blend.

This dish works well with cooked left over white chicken meat.

*Quick cook chicken method: boil 1 cup chicken stock - low sodium, add chopped chicken, cover and simmer for 5 minutes. Drain chicken and allow cooling for few minutes.

Orzo Chicken Salad

Prep: 10 min - Cook: 10 min - Chill: 60 Min - Serves Six

Ingredients:

1 cup orzo pasta - uncooked

1lb. chicken breast - cooked - diced

1/2 cup red onion - diced

1/2 cup green bell pepper - diced

1/2 cup red bell pepper - diced

1/2 cup red bell pepper - diced

1 cup cherry tomatoes - halved

1 tablespoon olive oil

Dressing: combine the following ingredients in a bowl:

1/4 cup mayonnaise - low fat

1/4 cup sour cream - low fat

1 tablespoon apple cider vinegar

1 tablespoon Dijon mustard

1 tablespoon yellow mustard

2 tablespoons fresh chives - chopped

1/2 teaspoon white sugar

salt and pepper to taste

Directions:

1. Cook pasta per package instructions. Rinse under cold water to cool.

2. Heat olive oil in skillet over medium heat and cook chicken for 5 minutes or until cooked. Set to side.

3. In a large bowl, combine the pasta, chicken, tomatoes, peppers and red onion. Add dressing and lightly toss.

4. Cover and chill till ready to serve.

Chicken Caesar Salad

Prep: 10 min - Cook: 15 min - Serves Four

Ingredients:

1 lb. chicken breast - cut into strips

1 1/2 cups croutons

1 cup Caesar dressing—low fat

1/4 cup parmesan cheese—grated

2 romaine lettuce - tear into bite size pieces

1 lemon—cut into 8 wedges

1 tablespoon olive oil

Combine the following ingredients in a small bowl:

1 1/2 teaspoons garlic salt

1 teaspoon lemon pepper seasoning

Directions:

1. Rub small bowl mix on chicken.

2. Heat olive oil in skillet over medium heat. Add chicken and cook for 10 - 15 minutes, or until cooked, stirring often.

3. Cut lettuce into bite size pieces and place in large bowl.

4. Add Caesar dressing, parmesan cheese and croutons to

lettuce. Toss until combined well.

5. Divide Caesar salad evenly on 4 plates.

6. Place cooked chicken strips on top of salad.

7. Garnish with 2 lemon wedges.

8. Cover and chill till ready to serve.

Rosemary Chicken Salad

Prep: 10 min - Cook: 10 min - Serves Four

Ingredients:

1 tablespoon olive oil

Combine the following ingredients in a bowl:

1 lb. chicken breast - cooked - cooled- chopped

1/4 cup green onions - chopped

1/4 cup almonds - chopped

1/4 cup yogurt - plain - fat free

1/4 cup mayonnaise - low fat

1 apple - peeled - cored - chopped

1 teaspoon fresh rosemary - chopped

1 teaspoon Dijon mustard

1/8 teaspoon salt

1/8 teaspoon black pepper

Directions:

1. Heat oil in skillet over medium heat; add chicken and sauté till cooked - about 5 minutes. Drain and let cool.

2. Combine all ingredients in a large bowl.

3. Add chicken to bowl, stir well.

4. Cover and chill till ready to serve.

.

Chicken Potato Salad

Prep: 15 min - Cook: 8 min - Serves Four

Ingredients:

1 lb. chicken breast - chopped

1 lb. potatoes - peeled and cubed

1 tablespoon olive oil

Combine the following ingredients in a bowl:

3/4 cup mayonnaise

1/2 cup grapes - chopped

1/3 cup celery - chopped

1/4 cup onion - chopped

1 apple - peeled and chopped

1 carrot - peeled and chopped

2 tablespoons sofrito

2 tablespoons lime juice

1 tablespoon olive oil

salt and ground black pepper to taste

Directions:

1. Boil cubed potatoes for 8 minutes, remove from heat,

drain and set to side to allow cooling.

2. Heat olive oil in skillet and cook chicken for 4 minutes or until cooked. Set to side.

3. Combine remaining ingredients in a bowl, add cooked chicken and cooked potatoes.

4. Cover and chill till ready to serve.

Chicken Asparagus Salad

Prep: 15 min - Cook: 10 min - Serves Four

Ingredients:

1 lb. chicken breast - cut into 1-inch cubes

8 cups mixed salad greens

12 oz. asparagus - cut into 2-inch pieces

1 cup cherry tomatoes - halved

1/2 cup water

1 tablespoon olive oil

Dressing: combine the following ingredients in a small bowl:

1/2 cup mayonnaise

1/2 cup sour cream

1/4 cup green onion - thinly sliced

1 tablespoon chopped fresh basil leaves

1 tablespoon lemon juice

1/4 teaspoon grated lemon peel

salt and ground black pepper to taste

Directions:

1. Make dressing and chill till ready to serve.

2. Heat olive oil in skillet and cook chicken for 5 minutes or until cooked. Set to side.

3. Bring to boil 1/2 cup water to boil in small saucepan, add asparagus, cover and cook for 4 minutes. Drain and rinse with cold water.

4. In a large salad bowl, combine greens, chicken and tomatoes. Arrange salad onto four plates and top with chilled dressing.

5. Cover and chill till ready to serve.

Cassie's Chicken Salad

Prep: 15 min - Serves Four

Ingredients:

1 lb. chicken breast - chopped

1 romaine lettuce - torn into bite size pieces

1 package (10 ounce) baby spinach

2 cups raspberries

3 tablespoons dried cranberries

3 tablespoons dried cherries

3 tablespoons dried apples

6 tbsp. Raspberry Vinaigrette

6 oz. Feta

1 tablespoon olive oil

Directions:

1. Heat olive oil in skillet over medium heat and cook chicken for 5 minutes or until cooked. Set to side.

2. Place lettuce, spinach, raspberries, cranberries, cherries and apple in a large bowl.

3. Add raspberry vinaigrette dressing to salad, toss to coat.

4. Divide salad onto 4 serving plates and top with

crumbled feta cheese.

5. Cover and chill till ready to serve.

Chicken Broth

Cook: 4 hours - Yield: 3 quarts

Ingredients:

3 pounds uncooked chicken wings

3 quarts water

1 large onion, chopped

2 garlic cloves - minced

1 teaspoon salt - or more to taste

1/4 teaspoon ground black pepper

2 bay leaves

Directions:

1. Place all ingredients in a large saucepan and bring to the boil, cover pan, then lower heat to lowest setting and simmer for 4 - 5 hours.

2. Strain out all the ingredients till your left with liquid only. More salt and pepper can be added to taste if needed.

3. Refrigerate to chill, then remove and fat from top.

You're chicken broth can be kept in refrigerator for up to 4 days, and can be frozen for up to 3 months.

Salsa

Prep: 10 min - Yield: 3-4 cups

Ingredients:

1 1/2 lb. tomatoes - stems removed - finely diced

1/2 red onion - finely diced

1 jalapeño chili pepper - stems, ribs, seeds removed - finely diced*

1 serrano chili pepper - stems, ribs, seeds removed - finely diced*

Juice of one lime

1/2 cup cilantro - chopped

1/4 teaspoon cumin

1/4 teaspoon oregano

Salt and pepper to taste

Directions:

1. Combine all of the ingredients in a bowl. If the chilies make the salsa too hot, add some more diced tomato.

2. Let sit for an hour at room temperature.

Guacamole

Prep: 20 min - Serves Six

Ingredients:

5 large hass avocadoes

1/4 cup lime juice - freshly squeezed

1 white onion - medium - chopped

2 tablespoons cilantro - chopped

1 large tomato - diced

1 garlic clove - minced

1/2 teaspoon kosher salt

1/2 teaspoon cumin

1/2 teaspoon cayenne

1/2 jalapeno pepper - seeded - finely chopped

Directions:

1. Put lime juice in a bowl.

2. Slice avocados in half, discard seed, scoop out of shell with a spoon and place into bowl. Mash avocados in lime juice right away to prevent browning.

3. Fold in all other ingredients, and then gently stir.

4. Let sit at room temperature for 30 minutes, then serve.

Mayonnaise

Prep: 5 min - Yield: 1 cup

Ingredients:

1 cup olive oil

1 egg yolk

2 teaspoons white wine vinegar

2 teaspoons lemon juice

1 teaspoon Dijon mustard

1/4 teaspoon kosher salt

Directions:

1. Put ingredients into a bowl and whisk till texture is thick.

Can be stored in in the refrigerator for up to several weeks.

Books in Colin's 'a cookbook' series:

SALMON a cookbook
LAMB a cookbook
CHICKEN BREAST a cookbook
SALAD a cookbook

http://www.amazon.com/Colin-Simpson/e/B00DYQNMGG

International conversions:

Cooking Measurement Conversions

1 teaspoon = 1/6 fl. Ounce

1 Tablespoon = 1/2 fl. Ounce

1 tablespoon = 3 teaspoons

1 dessert spoon (UK) = 2.4 teaspoons

16 tablespoons = 1 cup

12 tablespoons = 3/4 cup

10 tablespoons + 2 teaspoons = 2/3 cup

8 tablespoons = 1/2 cup

6 tablespoons = 3/8 cup

5 tablespoons + 1 teaspoon = 1/3 cup

4 tablespoons = 1/4 cup

2 tablespoons = 1/8 cup

2 tablespoons + 2 teaspoons = 1/6 cup

1 tablespoon = 1/16 cup

2 cups = 1 pint

2 pints = 1 quart

3 teaspoons = 1 tablespoon

48 teaspoons = 1 cup

1 cup = 8 fluid ounces

2 cups= 1 pint

2 cups= 16 fluid ounces

1 quart = 2 pints

4 cups = 1 quart

4 cups = 32 fluid ounces

8 cups = 4 pints

8 cups = 1/2 gallon

8 cups = 64 fluid ounces

4 quarts =1 gallon

4 quarts = 128 fluid ounces
1 gallon (gal) = 4 quarts
16 ounces = 1 pound
Pinch = Less than 1/8 teaspoon

Fahrenheit to Celsius Degrees Conversions

225F = 110C = Gas mark 1/4
250F = 120C = Gas mark 1/2
275F = 140C = Gas mark 1
300F = 150C = Gas mark 2
325F = 160C = Gas mark 3
350F = 180C = Gas mark 4
375F = 190C = Gas mark 5
400F = 200C = Gas mark 6
425F = 220C = Gas mark 7
450F = 230C = Gas mark 8
475F = 240C = Gas mark 9

Imperial to Metric Conversions

1/4 teaspoon = 1.25 ml
1/2 tsp = 2.5 ml
1 tsp = 5 ml
1 tablespoon = 15 ml
1/4 cup = 60 ml
1/3 cup = 75 ml
1/2 cup = 125 ml
2/3 cup = 150 ml
3/4 cup = 175 ml
1 cup = 250 ml
1 1/8 cups = 275 ml
1 1/4 cups = 300 ml

1 1/2 cups = 350 ml
1 2/3 cups = 400 ml
1 3/4 cups = 450 ml
2 cups = 500 ml
2 1/2 cups = 600 ml
3 cups = 750 ml
3 2/3 cups = 900 ml
4 cups = 1 liter

Weight Conversion

1/2 oz = 15g
1 oz = 25 g
2 oz = 50 g
3 oz = 75 g
4 oz = 100 g
6 oz = 175 g
7 oz = 200 g
8 oz = 250 g
9 oz = 275 g
10 oz = 300 g
12 oz = 350 g
1 lb = 500 g
1 1/2 = 750 g
2 lb = 1 kg

CPSIA information can be obtained
at www.ICGtesting.com
Printed in the USA
LVHW080139210420
654150LV00010B/3107